F
R
xxx .

the Visiting Book

Adventures in Yorkshire & North Lincolnshire

By

Rebecca Dennison

DAISA & CO
PUBLISHING

The Visiting Book published in Great Britain in 2019
Written & Illustrated by Rebecca Dennison
Copyright © Rebecca Dennison 2019

A CIP catalogue record for this book is available from the British Library

Paperback ISBN 978-1-9162023-4-4

Book Cover Design by: Rebecca Dennison & Daisa & Co Publishing,
Cover Image © Rebecca Dennison 2019

Book typeset by:
DAISA & CO PUBLISHING
Barton Upon Humber
North Lincolnshire
United Kingdom
DN18 5JR
www.daisapublishing.com

Printed in England

Daisa & Co Publishing is committed to a sustainable future for our business, our readers and our planet.

This book is made from paper certified by the Forestry Stewardship Council (FSC), an organisation dedicated to promoting responsible management of forest resources.

HOW to uSe this BOOK

you will need
(all these are optional)

A pen and coloured pencils
add colour to all the places you visit

& GLUE for sticking things in

FRIENDS
(FURRY OR HUMAN)
FAMILY OR
JUST YOURSELF
spend time with real humans and animals breathing lovely fresh air

using the postcode find the distance to each place from YOUR LOCATION

GOOGLE MAPS
(or a paper one)

a picnic
but there are lots of opportunities for cake.

Pennies and some POUNDS
lots of attractions are free but not all of them

The left hand side of this book is for

YOU

fill it with your pictures, memories of your visits or things you would like to remember for next time!

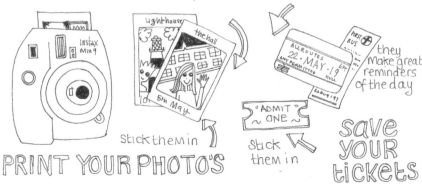

they make great reminders of the day

PRINT YOUR PHOTO'S
stick them in

ADMIT ONE
stick them in

save YOUR tickets

Length of Journey by

car

on foot

The artisan

Hull

HU5 2AL

LOCATED ON NEWLAND AVENUE THE ARTISAN IS A
COFFEE SHOP WITH A HEART. SERVING DELICIOUS
FOOD AND DRINK AND SUPPORTING LOCAL ARTISTS.
THANKYOU TO EMMA HER TEAM AND CUSTOMERS
FOR ALL THEIR SUPPORT ♥

Length of Journey by [car] [on foot]

Danes Dyke

Bridlington
YO15 1AA

PICNIC PERFECT

DOG FRIENDLY

OPEN ALL YEAR

FREE

TOILETS
PAY AND DISPLAY CARPARK
CAFE

Length of Journey by [car] [on foot]

Brantingham Dale

Lovely Walks for Humans and Dogs

HU15 1QJ

• EAST YORKSHIRE •

Length of Journey by [car] [on foot]

Length of Journey by   car   on foot

Burton agnes Hall

BURTON AGNES – DRIFFIELD
YO25 4NE

BEAUTIFUL HALL AND GARDENS

CHARGES MAY APPLY
CHECK ONLINE

Length of Journey by [car] [on foot]

the Piece Hall

HALIFAX

HX1 1RE

INDEPEDENT SHOPS, CAFES
AND BARS

ART GALLERY

HERITAGE VISITORS CENTRE

FOR OPENING TIMES CHECK ONLINE

WELL BEHAVED DOGS WELCOME IN SOME AREAS CHECK ONLINE

Length of Journey by   car   on foot

[ ] [ ]

Castle Howard

18th century House and Estate

YO60 7DA

check website for opening times and charges

Length of Journey by [car] [on foot]

flamborough head

YO15 1AR

NORTH LANDING - COASTAL WALK
PERFECT FOR DOGS

LIGHTHOUSE
VISITORS
CENTRE

ROCK POOLING

CHARGES MAY APPLY CHECK ONLINE FOR DETAILS

Length of Journey by car on foot

Nutwood & WAULDBY SCROGS
(Bluebell Wood)

HU16 5YL

free

CAN BE MUDDY

OPPOSITE RAYWELL HALL

A LOVELY WOOD FOR WALKS AND DEN BUILDING FAMILY AND DOG FRIENDLY

Length of Journey by car   on foot

A Labyrinth of tunnels, chambers follies and surprises!

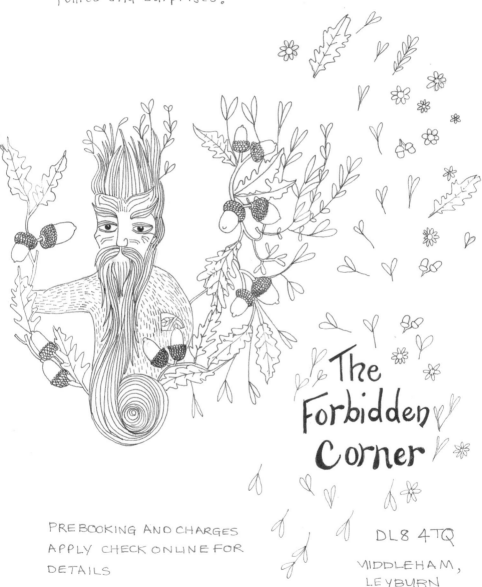

The Forbidden Corner

PRE BOOKING AND CHARGES APPLY CHECK ONLINE FOR DETAILS

DL8 4TQ

MIDDLEHAM, LEYBURN

Length of Journey by [car] [on foot]

Length of Journey by [car] [on foot]

course

Puffins

YO15 1JF

Bempton Cliffs

Nature reserve

seabird centre

charges apply check online

Length of Journey by [car] [on foot]

salts mill

... SALTAIRE ...

independant retail, Cafes and Gallery

BD17 7EF

1853 GALLERY

SALTS

David HOCKNEY

coffee

Shop

Length of Journey by car on foot

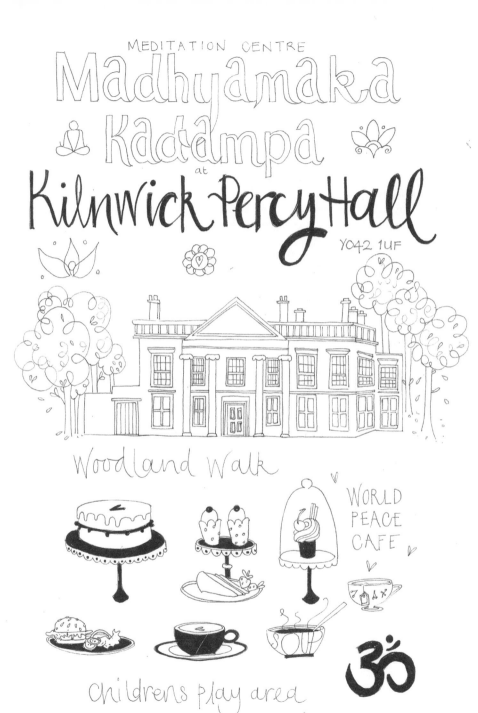

MEDITATION CENTRE

Madhyamaka
Kadampa
at
Kilnwick Percy Hall

YO42 1UF

Woodland Walk

WORLD PEACE CAFE

Childrens play area

CHECK ONLINE FOR OPENING TIMES

Length of Journey by   car   on foot

[   ]   [   ]

Millington Wood
and Millington Pastures

YO42 1TX

POCKLINGTON

walk

The Rambler's Rest
TEA ROOM & RESTAURANT

Length of Journey by [car] [on foot]

NR
HULL

the Humber Bridge

HU13 0HB

& Country Park

(LITTLE SWITZERLAND)

-EXPLORE-
- WALK-
-SKIM STONES-
-PUB LUNCH-
-ICE CREAM-
- PARK -
- RUN -

FREE

Length of Journey by [car] [on foot]

NORMANBY

DN15 9HU
NORMANBY
NR SCUNTHORPE

& COUNTRY
PARK

HALL

Tea Room

Farming Museum

check website for opening
times and charges

Length of Journey by [car] [on foot]

fraisethorpe beach

(near Bridlington)   YO15 3QU

parking charges apply   dog friendly

Length of Journey by [car] [on foot]

Hornsea by the Sea

Museum HU18 1AB

Mere HU18 1AX

freeport HU18 1UT

Beach HU18 1PZ

for charges and opening times please check website

Length of Journey by [car] [on foot]

Mallyan Spout

YO22 5LX

GOATHLAND

BECK

WOODLAND WALK

VISIT A HERMITAGE

TEA GARDEN CAFE

POOH
STICKS

May Beck and falling foss

NR WHITBY

CHILD
FRIENDLY

MAGICAL WOODLAND WALK - YO22 5JD

Length of Journey by car [ ] on foot [ ]

Hull Marina

HU1 2DQ

LEARN

WALK

ART

GALLERIES

SHOP

DEAD BOD

EAT

PARKING CHARGES MAY APPLY

Length of Journey by [car] [on foot]

SPURN POINT

HUMBER ESTUARY

HU12 0UH

SPURN SAFARI
(PRE-BOOK)

CYCLE HIRE
(I. D. REQUIRED)

CAFE

charges apply and opening hours vary check
online for more details

Length of Journey by   car [ ]   on foot [ ]

SEWERBY HALL AND GARDENS

YO15 1EA

BRIDLINGTON

HELLO!

ZOO

ACTUAL TALKING PARROTS

LAND TRAIN TO BRIDLINGTON

charges apply check online for details

Length of Journey by [car] [on foot]

YO22 4SJ

Robin Hoods Bay

NR WHITBY

Visit the old coastguard station

Beach & Coastal Walk

Cream Tea

Length of Journey by   car [ ]   on foot [ ]

CUSWORTH
HALL
MUSEUM

DN5 7TU

and park

Walk

TeaRoom

— PICNIC —

FREE ADMISSION

Parking charges apply

Length of Journey by [car] [on foot]

the Yorkshire sculpture park

WF4 4JX

Gallery   Shop   Cafe

PARKING CHARGES APPLY CHECK ONLINE FOR DETAILS.

Length of Journey by [car] [on foot]

Barton

UPON HUMBER

FREE (voluntary donations welcome)

Baysgarth House
Museum

DN18 6AH

The
King
Corridor

DN18 5QP

Wilderspin National school

Length of Journey by [car] [on foot]

the
ROPEWALK

BARTON

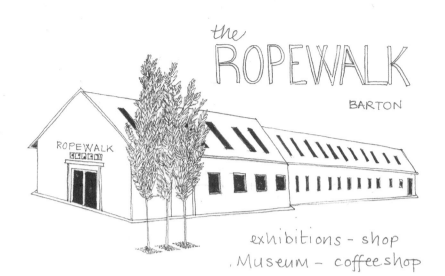

exhibitions - shop
. Museum - coffee shop

FREE

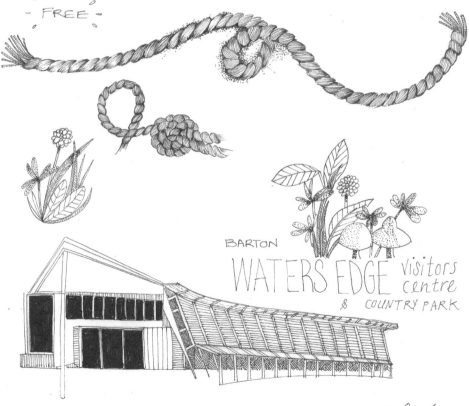

BARTON
WATERS EDGE visitors centre
& COUNTRY PARK

Cafe   Walks

Length of Journey by [car] [on foot]

TRINITY
T M
MARKET
19 04

HULL
OLD TOWN

HU1 2JH

ENTERTAINMENT – POP UPS – SHOP – SOCIAL

FALAFAL

T

ECO

PIZZA

YUM!

CHECK ONLINE FOR OPENING TIMES AND EVENTS

Length of Journey by [car] [on foot]

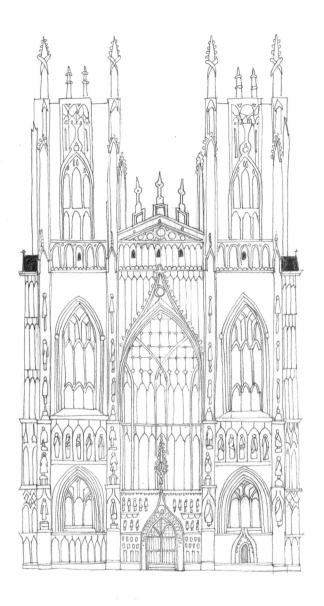

Beverley
Minster
HU17 0DP
EAST - YORKSHIRE

BUILDING TOURS (FEE AND
BOOKING APPLY)

ART EXHIBITIONS & FAIRS

CONCERTS

CHECK ONLINE FOR DETAILS

Length of Journey by [car] [on foot]

POCKLINGTON, E. YORKSHIRE

BURnby Hall

GARDENS

NATIONAL COLLECTION
OF WATER LILLIES
(MID-JUNE-AUGUST)

Secret

Nymphaea

Garden

The Stewart
Museum

CHARGES APPLY CHECK ONLINE FOR DETAILS

Length of Journey by | car | on foot

Brimham Rocks

HG3 4DW

SUMMERBRIDGE , HARROGATE

- an area of outstanding beauty -

Parking charges apply - check online for details.

Length of Journey by   car [ ]   on foot [ ]

UNIVERSITY OF HULL HU6 7RX

science fair
CHECK ONLINE FOR DATES

sculptures
↳ cairns
Moth↘
Toads

ART GALLERY

enjoy a campus walk

a nice cuppa

Beautiful Gardens

* WHY NOT TAKE A WALK ONTO NEWLAND PARK AND SEE LARKINS HOUSE AND TOAD! *

Length of Journey by [car] [on foot]

MARKET WEIGHTON

YO43 3AR
FREE PARKING AVAILABLE

2 PLAY PARKS

THE FOOTPRINT
OF
WILLIAM BRADLEY
THE TALLEST
ENGLISHMAN
EVER RECORDED
IN THIS HOUSE
BORN

FOLLOW THE
GIANT BRADLEY
TRAIL
(download the PDF from
visithullandeastyorkshire.com)

VISIT ALL SAINTS CHURCH

CAN YOU FIND THE 7 CARVED MICE
BY THE FAMOUS THOMPSON STUDIO
OF KILBURN

CAFES

Length of Journey by [car] [on foot]

HUI2 8FP

(NAPOLEONIC FORTRESS)

PAULL NR HULL

FULL SIZE

ON DISPLAY

CHARGES APPLY CHECK ONLINE FOR DETAILS

Length of Journey by [car] [on foot]

Scarborough Castle

SCARBOROUGH
YO11 1HY

CHARGES APPLY CHECK ONLINE FOR DETAILS

St Marys Church

BURIEL PLACE OF ANNE BRONTE

YO11 1HY

CHECK ONLINE FOR OPENING TIMES

Length of Journey by   car   on foot

Paragon Arcade

HULL
HU1 3PQ

INDEPENDANT SHOPS AND LATE NIGHT EVENTS

CHECK ONLINE FOR OPENING TIMES AND EVENT DETAILS

Length of Journey by [car] [on foot]

SCUNTHORPE

2021

visual arts centre

DN15 6TB

PARKING NEARBY - CHARGES APPLY

SHOP · EXHIBITIONS · CAFE · FREE ENTRY

CHECK ONLINE FOR EVENT PROGRAMME

food and Drink
SOUP

Length of Journey by   car [   ]   on foot [   ]

Burton Constable Hall
HU11 4LN

Visit the House
GREAT HALL
CABINET OF CURIOSITIES
DINING ROOM
CHINESE ROOM
ETC

Gardens, Stables, Parkland
LOVELY WALKS . FAIRS . PICNICS

CHARGES APPLY CHECK ONLINE FOR DETAILS.

Length of Journey by [car] [on foot]

Sheffield Industrial Museums Trust

· abbeydale Industrial Hamlet · S7 2QW

· Shepherd Wheel workshop · S11 2YE

THE MILLOWNERS ARMS

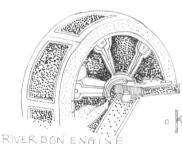

RIVER DON ENGINE

· Kelham Island Museum · S3 8RY

CHECK ONLINE FOR OPENING TIMES AND CHARGES

Length of Journey by   car   on foot

york

CITY

Walls

WALK

yorkwalls.org.uk

YO1 6HD

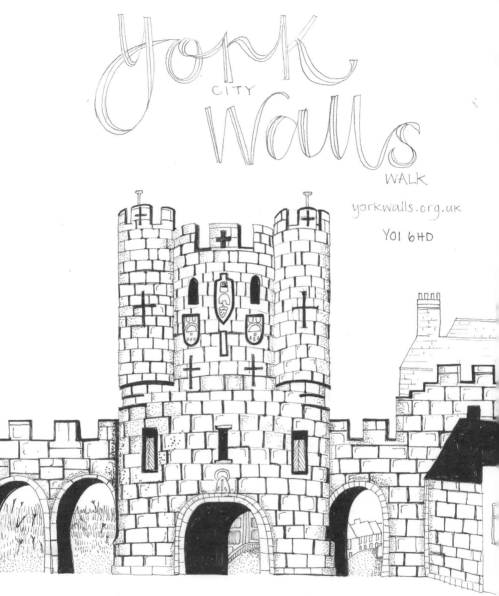

·· a stunning way to see YORK ··
the walk is 3·4 kilometres long
and takes about 2 hours, and
is ·FREE·

Length of Journey by   car   on foot

THE HEPWORTH WAKEFIELD

WFI 5AW

FREE ENTRY

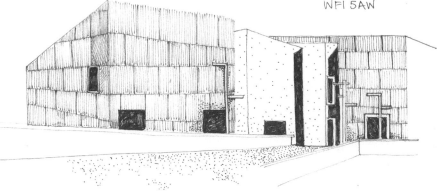

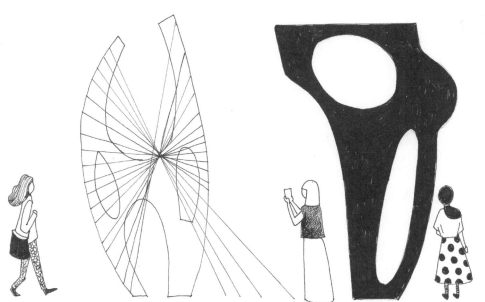

SHOP   CAFE   ART   SCULPTURES   FAIRS   LEARN   PLAY

PARKING CHARGES APPLY - CHECK ONLINE

Length of Journey by car [   ] on foot [   ]

RUDSTON

MONOLITH

(NR DRIFFIELD)

YO25 4UY

THE TALLEST MEGALITH IN THE U.K.
(A MEGALITH IS A PREHISTORIC MONUMENT)

A LOVELY WALK

VISIT ALL SAINTS CHURCH

Length of Journey by [car] [on foot]

YORKSHIRE DALES
CLAPHAM AND
INGLEBOROUGH

LA2 2EE

CAVES

CHARGES APPLY - CHECK ONLINE FOR DETAILS

Length of Journey by [car] [on foot]

YORKSHIRE DALES
BOLTON ABBEY
ANCIENT RUINS

OPENING TIMES CHANGE THROUGH
THE YEAR - CHECK ONLINE

323 6EX

RIVER WHARFE

CHARGES APPLY - CHECK ONLINE

Length of Journey by [car] [on foot]

Yorkshire Wildlife Park

DN4 6TB

FOR CHARGES, EVENTS AND OPENING TIMES CHECK ONLINE

Length of Journey by [car] [on foot]

Mother

Shipton's

CAVE

CHARGES APPLY CHECK ONLINE FOR DETAILS

Length of Journey by [car] [on foot]

WORSBROUGH MILL

S70 SLJ   **BARNSLEY**

COUNTRY PARK • FOX WALK • BADGER WALK • • OWL WALK •

FREE ADMISSION

WATCH FLOUR BEING MILLED

LEARN

BUY!

Length of Journey by [car] [on foot]

HUI IPS

street Life

TRANSPORT MUSEUM
HULL

REQUEST

WESTDOCK 216

5

KKH65

HANDS ON EXHIBITS

FAMILY FRIENDLY

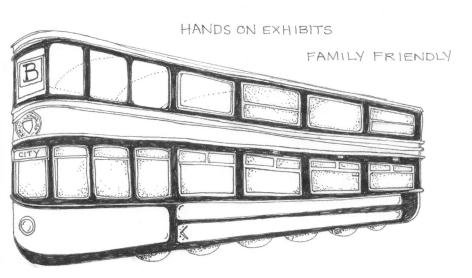

B

CITY

FREE ENTRY

Length of Journey by [car] [on foot]

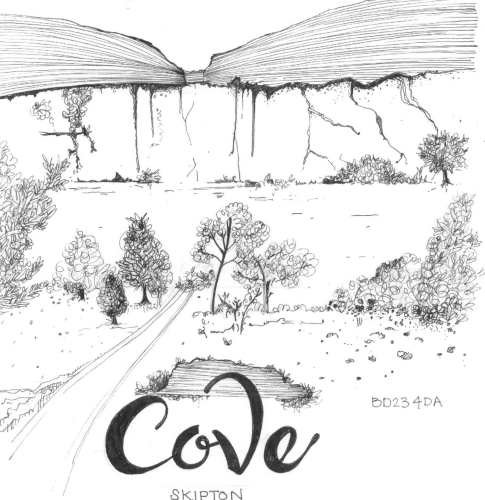

Malham
♥ YORKSHIRE DALES ♥

Cove
SKIPTON

BD23 4DA

PARKING CHARGES APPLY CHECK ONLINE · FOR DETAILS

Length of Journey by car | on foot |

POTTER ABOUT HORNSEA

HU18 1AB

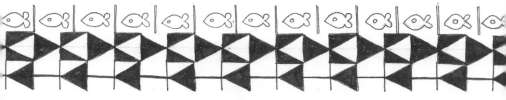

CELEBRATION OF HORNSEA POTTERY
SELF GUIDED ART TRAIL

DOWNLOAD THE TRAIL MAP AT HORNSEAMUSEUM.COM ꞏFREEꞏ

Length of Journey by [car] [on foot]

BOGGLE HOLE

WHITBY. NORTH. YORKS.

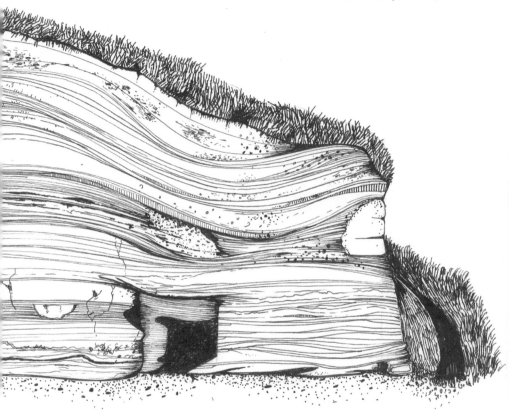

A Boggle is the local name for a hobgoblin, the mischievous little people that were thought to live in caves along the coast as well as the more remote corners of the Moors.

BOGGLE HOLE WAS THE PLACE SMUGGLERS USED TO LAND THEIR CONTRABAND

= FREE =

Length of Journey by [car] [on foot]

Lambing Sundays

in
— April —

Dates vary each year - check online.
!start looking in March for details!

BAA

BISHOP BURTON COLLEGE & ELSHAM HALL

BEVERLEY - HU17 8QD   BRIGG - DN20 0QZ

Length of Journey by [car] [on foot]

Elsham Hall

Hall · Gardens · Country Park

animals & Tea Room

CHARGES APPLY CHECK ONLINE

DN20 0QZ

BRIGG, Nth. LINCOLNSHIRE

Length of Journey by [car] [on foot]

Sledmere House

DRIFFIELD
YO25 3XG

House   Gardens   stables   playpark

Length of Journey by [car] [on foot]

THACKRAY MEDICAL MUSEUM LEEDS

An interactive Museum telling the story of medicine from Victorian times until now

Length of Journey by [car] [on foot]

SEAL SEASON - NOVEMBER - DECEMBER

Donna Nook

LN11 7PD - LOUTH - NORTH LINCOLNSHIRE

:FREE:

PARKING CHARGES MAY APPLY CHECK ONLINE RESERVE OPEN ALL YEAR

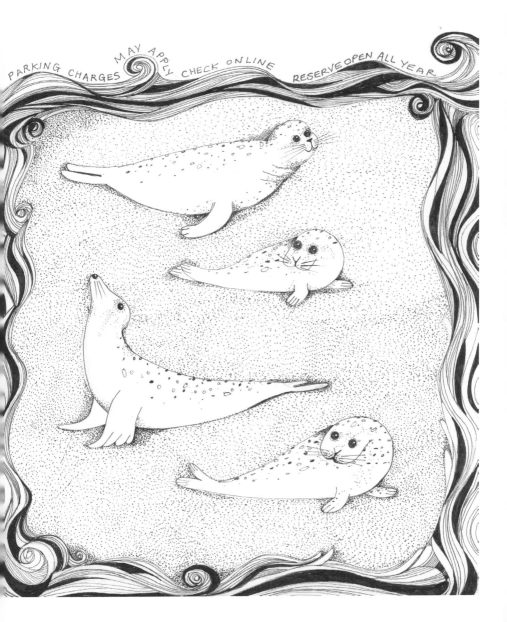

Length of Journey by [car] [on foot]

Brodsworth Hall

DNS 7XJ

ENTRY FEE APPLIES CHECK ONLINE FOR DETAILS

Length of Journey by [car] [on foot]

HULL HU2 8AG

sjar

skeg

OUTDOOR GALLERY LOCATED ON AN INDUSTRIAL ESTATE ALONG THE RIVER HULL

Length of Journey by [car] [on foot]

NATIONAL SCIENCE AND MEDIA MUSEUM

BRADFORD
BD1 1NQ

IMAX® CINEMA

WONDERLAB

PRODUCTION

DIRECTOR

| SCENE | TAKE | ROLL |

DATE

FREE ENTRY - VOLUNTARY DONATIONS WELCOME - ACTIVITY CHARGES APPLY
CHECK ONLINE BEFORE VISITING

Length of Journey by [car] [on foot]

National Coalmining Museum
for England

WF4 4RH

OVERTON, WAKEFIELD

FREE

MINE TOURS
SHOULD BE BOOKED
IN ADVANCE. A CHARGE
MAY APPLY - CHECK ONLINE

Length of Journey by [car] [on foot]

HENRY MOORE INSTITUTE

LS1 3AA

LEEDS CITY GALLERY

FREE ENTRY - SHOP AND CAFE

Length of Journey by [car] [on foot]

YO26 4XJ

The National Railway Museum

YORK

MALLARD

4468

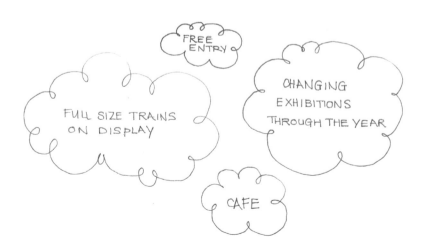

FREE ENTRY

CHANGING EXHIBITIONS THROUGH THE YEAR

FULL SIZE TRAINS ON DISPLAY

CAFE

CHARGES MAY APPLY FOR SOME ACTIVITIES, CHECK ONLINE

Length of Journey by [car] [on foot]

Skipsea

COASTAL WALK

MR MOO'S

♡ ICE - CREAM PARLOUR ♡

YO25 8SY

CHECK ONLINE FOR OPENING TIMES AND PRICES

This Book is Dedicated to those that saw its Potential

MY HUSBAND DENNY AND DAUGHTERS ELLIE & EVIE & MY MUM & DAD

♥ Thankyou ♥

My Kickstarter backers & MRS GLENIS WALTERS

MICHELLE & MIKE SANDERS
SOPHIE WHITTLE
ASH HARDISTER
MELVYN MARRIOTT
CHRISTINE HILL
LUCY GODWIN
LAURA INGHAM
MAE YEN
CENTRAL HUB TEAM
DEBRA RAMSEY
NIKKI DAVIES
HANNEKE WOOD
OLGA IVANOVA
GARY SHAW
ANGELA HODGSON
CLARE OMISSI
SHARON MARKHAM
SAM NABB
RACHEL CARROLL
RADIO HUMBERSIDE
THE CONLEY FAMILY

JO
EMMA PALMER
KATHRYN AC
DAVID PAFFLEY
SUZY DRAKE-DAVIS
JANE MANN
HANNAH WOODS
ANITA McGARRY
WINNIE HEGARTY-PEGDEN
MARGARET LEWIS
SARAH LILLEYMAN
HELEN LEVITT
DANNY FINN
LIZ CAGNEY
AMY RICHARDSON
DANIEL CORBIN
RICH SUTHERLAND
JENI DAY
TOM WATTS
OLIVIA AT BURTON AGNES HALL
LORRAINE SNEDDON

HANNAH LANGTHORPE
JESSIE HOWARD
CLARE BURMAN
SALLY FAIRFAX
TAMANA BLEASDALE
MELANIE MORGAN
BETH FEATHERSTONE
SAM TILLISON
LUCY BIGGS
MARIA PROUDLEY
EVA GORSKI
MARGARET WILSON
BRIAN HOLT
THERESA BROOKFIELD
CLARE STOCKER
BIANCA MOONE
RICHARD VAUGHAN
MICHELLE HAMPSON
HAZEL SIVORI
SUE

ADAM PAFFLEY
RACHEL HACKFORD
JENNA TRAIN
GINA RAYMENT
NICOLA
DANA FAINARU
GAVIN PUGH
CLAIRE MIDGLEY
SUZIE O'CONNOR
PAM MEDHURST
LEONORE SUTHERLAND
AMY MOORE
COLLETTE BRAITHWAITE
VANESSA LEE
SARAH HAMMOND
MICHAEL EWEN
TRACY PARK
PAUL FIRTH
LUCY STOBBS
SANDRA STOKES

ALISON WOOD
EMMA SUNMAN
CLARE BECKWITH
REBECCA DENNETT
CASSIE KEMP
GWYNETH PAFFLEY
STACY HOPKINSON
STACY KITE
VICKY WALMSLEY
ELIZABETH PEARSON
FIONA LEVITT
EMMA CHADWICK
LIZ
LIZ HOBSON
DION COE
EMMA BANNIGAN
STEWART WILSON
COLETTE BURROUGHS-ROSE
GUEST BACKERS!
ANJI GARDENER

BV - #0016 - 021219 - C0 - 210/148/7 - PB - 9781916202344